ENGAGE IN SPIRITUAL DISCIPLINES

vi+al:PRAYER WITNESSING FASTING LIVING FOR TODAY

PHIN HALL

CWR

Contents:

Introduction:

> 'I have fought the good fight, I have finished the race, I have kept the faith. Now there is in store for me the crown of righteousness, which the Lord, the righteous Judge, will award to me on that day.'
> **2 Timothy 4:7–8**

A fight and a race. This is how Paul described his life as a Christian. Of course, these are not the *only* images he used, in fact the most common was that of a family, with God as the father and with the Church being full of His children – an important emphasis since, above all else, Christianity is about relationships. No matter what else it may involve, Christianity is essentially about having a loving relationship with God. This is the great privilege and joy of being one of God's people – part of His family.

That said, Paul's comparison of Christian life with a fight and a race is also appropriate. After all, love for God is not something that simply appears, fully mature, overnight. As with any other relationship, it takes time and effort to grow and to develop, working together with God. God's role is to 'change our hearts', bringing our desires and attitudes more in line with His own. Our role is to engage in spiritual discipline – in practices that have been used by men and women of God throughout history and which have proved vital for building relationships with Him and with others. In this series we will look at the following areas of spiritual discipline that have stood the test of time:

+ **Focus on God:** worship, Bible study, meditation and prayer.

+ **Focus on others:** fellowship, submission, serving and witnessing.

+ **Focus on ourselves:** simplicity, giving, battling
  temptation and fasting.

+ **Focus on daily life:** solitude, silence, giving thanks,
  confession and living for today.

This is our fight. This is our race. And like any fight or
race, if they are truly to make a difference we need to
persevere and go the distance!

Consider marriage. Husbands and wives use tools
such as good communication and spending quality
time together to build their relationship, but even the
best of marriages will start to fall apart if that effort is
not maintained. Good marriages take time and effort
'till death us do part'.

And when it comes to our relationship with God,
simply spending a few weeks trying out some areas of
spiritual discipline will have little effect in growing our
love for Him unless we persevere in them and press on
toward the goal to 'receive the crown of life that God
has promised to those who love him' (James 1:12).

In this book we will consider the following four areas:
prayer, witnessing, fasting and *living for today.* Each week
consists of five sessions of individual study, reflection and
application, with a sixth session of questions either for
personal consideration or group discussion.

My prayer is that these studies will help us as we persevere,
'going the distance' in our relationship with God.

See notes on page 55.

1. Read 1 Timothy 4:16, Hebrews 10:36 and James 1:12. Why do you think perseverance is so important for us in our relationship with God?

2. How would you explain the purpose and practice of prayer?

3. How would you explain the purpose and practice of witnessing?

4. How would you explain the purpose and practice of fasting?

5. How would you explain the purpose and practice of living for today?

6. Which of these have you engaged in for any significant length of time and how have they helped your spiritual growth?

7. In what ways have you had to persevere in other relationships, whether in the home, at work or in your local church? How do they compare with those at which you have not continued to work?

WEEK 1: FOCUS ON GOD
prayer

PRAYER

www.cwr.org.uk/vital

Introduction

'Then Jesus told his disciples a parable to show them that they should always pray and not give up.' **Luke 18:1**

When it comes to spiritual discipline, prayer is one of the 'biggies' – easily up there with Bible study as the best known, if not necessarily the most practised. While there may be a little confusion over exactly what is involved in areas of discipline like Christian meditation, simplicity or other less common disciplines, we all know how to pray. Or do we? And if we do, does this result in us actually engaging in prayer?

While prayer is a fairly simple concept, in practice it is hard work. Even with all Jesus' teaching on prayer, His disciples still struggled to pray. And they are joined by countless others. To quote Dr Martyn Lloyd Jones: 'Everything we do in the Christian life is easier than prayer.'

Despite this, Jesus called His followers to 'always pray and not give up', and Paul went further with the command, 'pray continually' (1 Thess. 5:17). Can God seriously be calling us to a life of struggling to pray incessantly? Is it even possible? And even if it is, can prayer really be *that* important?

In this first week of studies, as we come to focus on God, we will be looking at what prayer is and why to do it, together with how to engage effectively in this spiritual discipline.

'When Moses entered the Tent of Meeting to speak with the LORD, he heard the voice speaking to him from between the two cherubim above the atonement cover on the ark of the Testimony. And he spoke with him.'
Numbers 7:89

prayer

Although this is a potentially vast topic, with many hundreds of books written on the subject, prayer is essentially very simple. It is speaking with God. The word 'with' plays an important role in this definition as listening is just as important an aspect of prayer as speaking – it is two-way communication, discussion and dialogue. So when we read that Moses spoke with the Lord in the tabernacle, we are reading about prayer. The only reason his conversations with *other* people could not be called prayer is that neither he nor they were God. Prayer is talking with God.

Usually, when people think of prayer, the emphasis is on asking God for things. Certainly the words for prayer in the Bible are primarily about making requests or even begging. This is even the root of our English word – consider Titania's request in Shakespeare's *A Midsummer Night's Dream*, 'I pray thee, mortal, sing again'. However, prayer is not restricted to presenting requests to God. When writing to Timothy, Paul listed a number of other types of prayer, 'I urge, then, first of all, that requests, prayers, intercession and thanksgiving be made for everyone' (1 Tim. 2:1) and many people have since sought to define types of prayer, inventing such impressive titles as 'prayers of consecration' and 'prayers of imprecation'. While these can be helpful reminders for us – once we have looked up what they mean! − no list can fully describe all aspects of prayer, just as it would be impossible to list all possible types of conversation.

One of the main barriers to engaging in prayer, though, is the tradition and ceremony that has been built around it. While putting our hands together and closing our eyes may help us to concentrate, and while kneeling and using particular forms of language may help us to focus, such things can easily turn prayer into a religious exercise that detracts and distracts us from simply talking with God. Imagine if every time I spoke to my mother I had to go through some rigmarole such as wearing a special hat, crawling on the floor and starting every sentence with 'O great fount of my being'. It would certainly make the whole exercise a bit complex and would undoubtedly lead to less communication. I would probably look pretty ridiculous too!

> < Reflection

I have a friend who only ever gets in contact with me when he wants something. Whether you could strictly class him as a 'friend', therefore, is difficult as our relationship never seems to get beyond this level and, sadly, I am not *always* thrilled to hear from him.

Making requests of God is certainly not a bad thing, but consider the effect on our relationship with Him if our prayers never progress beyond this.

'Let us then approach the throne of grace with confidence, so that we may receive mercy and find grace to help us in our time of need.'

Hebrews 4:16

prayer

The Israelites knew they were God's people. After all, it was God who had brought them out of slavery in Egypt, sending plagues, parting the Red Sea and destroying Pharaoh's army. It was God who had appeared to them in fire and smoke at Mount Sinai. And it was God who had filled the tabernacle in a great demonstration of His glory. But even though He dwelled in their midst, He did so cut off behind a curtain, hidden away inside a tent, and later in the temple, where only the priests could enter. The Israelites were God's people alright, but they could not approach Him fully – they did not have direct access to the presence of God.

This continued right up to the day Jesus was crucified. Then, as He offered up His life, everything changed: 'At that moment the curtain of the temple was torn in two from top to bottom' (Matt. 27:51). That great symbol of separation was ripped apart. Thanks to Jesus, people could finally approach God completely, without any barriers or obstacles! So, unlike the Israelites who got as close as they could but were always kept at a distance, we now have full, unlimited access to God. We can come to Him, with nothing to hold us back, to make our requests, to seek forgiveness, to ask for advice and guidance, to share our thoughts and to find refuge.

Imagine if we were granted full access to the prime minister. If we really wanted to use that access and speak with him, we would only do so if we had something really important and worthwhile to say. But it would be a mistake to apply this same restriction to our prayer lives. The Bible describes us as God's children, 'born of God' (John 1:13). He is not only interested in the things we might consider big or important, but He is our Father and He is interested in every aspect of our lives.

Jesus sacrificed everything to provide us with these wonderful privileges – not only to save us so that we get to go to heaven, but so that we who have trusted in Him can come to God in prayer, as children coming to our Father.

Application »

Only two men are referred to in the Bible as God's friends: Abraham and Moses. Read the following verses that give us examples of how they spoke with God – Genesis 18:23–33 and Exodus 4:1–15. Note how they both engaged in conversation with God, listening to and responding to Him. They did not use any special, holy words nor did they hide their true feelings away, but they were clear about the things that really mattered to them.

Spend some time today in prayer talking with God, as you would with a friend, about the things that really matter to you.

Communication Skills

'Those who are led by the Spirit of God are sons of God.'
Romans 8:14

prayer

A few years ago, police found a man lying in a pool of his own blood having tried to perform surgery on himself with a kitchen knife. When he was later asked about his actions, he explained, 'God told me that I had a religious medal in my stomach and that I should get it out with a knife before the world burst'! He, like so many others who have claimed to hear from God, is currently in a psychiatric hospital.

Suggesting you can hear God's voice is a dangerous thing – even more so if you act on it. And yet, as Christians, we believe that the opposite is true, and we *long* to be able to hear and recognise God's voice, often with the specific aim of acting upon it. Unfortunately, being able to discern when God is speaking to us is not that easy, and so much that is called prayer tends to be a rather one-sided exercise with us delivering a monologue to God, stamped with an 'Amen' and left at that. But to really engage in this area of spiritual discipline we need to speak *with* God, conversing and communicating with Him, listening to His voice as well as using our own.

While God can speak to us in many ways, such as through dreams, visions and the Bible, the most common way is directly into our thoughts. The real problem, then, is not *hearing* God's voice, but *recognising* it. Our thoughts all tend to sound fairly similar and it can be hard to distinguish between God's voice and our own, or even the voices of our spiritual enemy. Hard, but not impossible, and there are a number of ways we can test to see if we have heard His voice correctly:

+ *Check it out against Scripture.* While the Bible may not give us a relevant verse for every situation, it does at least give us a sense of how God speaks – the sort of things He says and the way He says them.

+ *Look for conviction,* which often accompanies the Holy Spirit's guidance.

+ If it involves making a fairly major decision (rather than just normal discussion) *check with wise, godly counsel* (see Prov. 12:15).

+ *Act on what you hear.* This may take us outside our comfort zone, but it can also reveal clearly if we have heard from God or not. And the more we test and work out when He has spoken to us, the better equipped we will be to recognise His voice in the future.

Application ››

Read John 10:1–5. Learning to discern God's voice among the jumble in our heads is hugely important if we are to follow His guidance and really build our relationship with Him. Take time each day for the rest of this week to ask God to bring someone to mind for whom to pray.

Having done so, let that person know you were praying for them and what you prayed about and see how he or she responds.

'The LORD would
speak to Moses face to
face, as a man speaks
with his friend.'
Exodus 33:11

prayer

There are roughly seven thousand spoken languages
in use around the world today. In addition to this there
are languages for those who cannot communicate
verbally – languages based on hand signs and on
touch. Though many people are concerned about
the breakdown of communication in modern society,
the reality is that we communicate more today, both
in quantity and range, than ever before thanks to the
the telephone, radio, email, texting and social media.
We do not communicate less, we communicate
differently – but we do communicate. Ultimately we
all crave the company of other people and thrive
on communication, and there are no relationships,
whether in the home, the workplace or in any other
context, that can survive without communication.
This is also true of our relationship with God.

Consider Moses, one of those the Bible refers to as
God's friend. We are told that He spoke with God face-
to-face, speaking and being spoken to, communicating
about both the little things and the big things, because
they were friends. Thanks to Jesus, such intimate
access to God has been given to us – we can come to
Him and speak with Him as we would with a friend.

When we speak with our friends we do so not only
when we have some important piece of information
to impart to them or a special request to make,

we chat with them about the big things and the little things, about situations that concern or excite us, about our plans, our dreams, our secrets, about everything and nothing. If we do not, can we really call them our friends? Speaking with God in the same open, expansive way is vital for our relationship with Him. Without it, we cannot ever hope to get beyond a merely superficial level, where God is little more than an acquaintance or a transcendent being that is somehow distant and cut off from us. Yet when we are disciplined in our prayer, taking the time to speak to God and listen to Him, we cannot help but grow in our relationship with Him. Communication is vital.

> < **Reflection**

Read Romans 8:9, 1 Corinthians 6:19 and 2 Timothy 1:14. Through these verses, a staggering truth is revealed about the intimacy and depth of relationship that is available to us as God's people. The Holy Spirit, who is God Himself, dwells in our bodies — somehow, in a very real sense, we share our bodies with God. What an amazing privilege!

When Jesus told His disciples about the work the Holy Spirit would do, almost every aspect involved some form of communication: reminding, teaching, guiding, speaking and making things known to us. The question is not, 'Does God speak to us?', but 'Do we take the time to listen and to respond, to speak with Him face-to-face as one speaks with a friend?'

'Going a little farther, he fell with his face to the ground and prayed, "My Father, if it is possible, may this cup be taken from me. Yet not as I will, but as you will."'

Matthew 26:39

The Gospel accounts are filled with examples of Jesus praying constantly, from His baptism through to the crucifixion. Even now, Paul tells us that He 'is at the right hand of God and is also interceding for us' (Rom. 8:34). When it comes to prayer, Jesus is the ultimate example. The disciples quickly realised this and asked Him: 'Lord, teach us to pray' (Luke 11:1), a request which resulted in Him teaching them the Lord's Prayer – a template that has been handed down to us through the centuries. He also used parables to teach on prayer, such as the Parable of the Persistent Widow (Luke 18:1-8), which made the point that prayer is not about trying to twist God's arm, but is about trusting Him and building our relationship with Him.

In these few studies on prayer, we have focused on *why* and *how* to pray, rather than *what* to pray, but it is worth considering the area of prayer requests as this tends to be the most common form of prayer.

Everyone wants God to answer their prayers – not with a 'no' or 'wait', but with a resounding 'yes!' – and the Bible is full of promises that God will grant the requests of His people. That said, it is also full of conditions to such promises, which imply God only grants requests for those things He was going to do anyway, which makes you wonder if it's really worth the hassle.

prayer

When Jesus was praying in the Garden of Gethsemane, minutes before He was arrested, He asked God to release Him from the suffering that lay ahead. Who wouldn't make such a request if placed in such a horrific situation? And yet, Jesus' request came with absolute submission to God's will. We cannot always know what God's will is and what He intends to do, so we should not consider our prayers a failure when our requests are not granted. Rather, if we follow Jesus' example and make our requests with open hands, trusting in and submitting to God's will, then our prayers make a difference whether they are granted or not.

Application »

Christians tend to make much of the fact that we can pray at anytime and in any place – we can pray in the car on the way to work, in the garden while hanging out the washing, even half way up a mountain if we happen to find ourselves in such a situation. The problem is that since we can pray wherever and whenever we like, it is all too easy to pray nowhere and never.

Take the time to look at your weekly schedule and book in set times of prayer to ensure you engage in this vital area of spiritual discipline.

1. What do you find hardest about praying – both when you pray alone and when you pray with others?

2. It is a sad fact that church prayer meetings are not well attended. Why do you think this is the case?

3. Read John 14:26 and 16:13. Note how many of the tasks the Holy Spirit is said to perform involve verbal communication. Have you experienced such communication from Him and how has this affected your walk with God?

4. When we take into account the various promises and conditions for getting our prayers 'answered' (i.e. getting our requests granted), the conclusion is that we need to ask in accordance with God's will. How could such prayers be considered worthwhile, since God would act in accordance with His will whether we ask Him or not?

5. Read John 10:1–5. Recognising God's voice is clearly important if we are to follow His guidance and not be led astray by other influences. How can we learn to discern when God is speaking and grow in our ability to recognise His voice?

6. How do prayer and meditation work together in helping our communication with God?

7. Many non-Christians assume that prayer involves certain physical postures and special holy words or that it is restricted to asking God for things. How would you explain the purpose and practice of prayer to such a person?

prayer

WEEK 2: FOCUS ON OTHERS
witnessing

Introduction

'He said to them, "Go into all the world and preach the good
news to all creation."'
Mark 16:15

Most Bibles note that the closing verses of Mark's Gospel were
probably not part of the original manuscript. As a result, there
has been a good deal of debate as to whether this command to
'preach the good news' still applies. However, while in this particular
instance we may be let off the hook, there are plenty of other
commands, such as the Great Commission (Matt 28:16–20) and
Jesus' parting words (Acts 1:1–8), that put us firmly back on it again.
If we are followers of Christ, we have been issued a clear command
to bear witness to the world around us that salvation is found in Him.

The problem is that, when it comes down to it, there are many
perceived obstacles that stand in the way of us telling other
people the good news about Jesus. 'What if someone asks me a
question and I don't know the answer?' 'How can I tell people I am
a Christian when my life doesn't quite match up to how a Christian
should live?' 'What if they attack me or worse, laugh at me?' Surely
it is best to leave it to those who have the gift of evangelism!

As we turn our attention to witnessing, we will be looking at
why this is an important task for all of us, together with what this
potentially risky area of spiritual discipline really involves.

Day 1
The Light of the World

witnessing

'In the same way, let your light shine before men, that they may see your good deeds and praise your Father in heaven.'
Matthew 5:16

One afternoon in 1992, as I was wandering home from college, I was almost run down by a guy on a motorbike. About five seconds later, the bike came to an abrupt stop. The rider, however, did not, and continued his reckless journey over the bonnet of the car he had hit and a short distance along the road beyond. From my vantage point I had seen the whole incident and was called on to be a witness to what had happened. And herein we can find three important principles involved in being a witness:

Firstly, *you need to know the truth*, by seeing, hearing or experiencing it yourself. I had seen the whole accident first hand – had I not, I would have been worthless as a witness. Before we can witness to others about Jesus, we need to know and be sure of the truth of the gospel. This means our experience of God's work in our lives is also of great value in our witnessing.

Secondly, *you need to be able to express the truth clearly and consistently.* If I had given garbled, conflicting statements about that accident, it would have been worthless. So too, when we testify to the truth about Christianity and God's work in our lives, we need to be able to communicate it in a way that is clear and consistent.

Finally, when it comes to being a witness in court, *character counts* – if I had been considered an unreliable witness, my testimony would have counted for nothing. Throughout Scripture, God's people are called to live in a way which is different from others, to be 'blameless and pure, children of God without fault in a crooked and depraved generation, in which you shine like stars in the universe as you hold out the word of life' (Phil. 2:15–16). We can hold out the word of life as much as we want, but people will not believe it if our lives fail to demonstrate that it is true.

There is a famous quote from Francis of Assisi which says, 'Preach the gospel at all times; when necessary, use words'. This does not mean we do not need to tell people the good news, but that the way we live should communicate it even more eloquently and convincingly than the things we say.

Application ››

Paul referred to the gospel as 'the power of God for the salvation of everyone who believes' (Rom. 1:16). This power is not confined to just a few points drawn from Scripture, but should have a continuous effect in all areas of our lives. Bearing witness to the power of the gospel in our daily lives can be a great tool for witnessing.

If you have never written a personal testimony, take the time to do so now – though it is important to remember that the gospel's effect in our lives is ongoing, providing us with new, powerful testimonies every day!

Making His Appeal Through Us

witnessing

'God our Saviour, who
wants all men to be
saved and to come to a
knowledge of the truth.'
1 Timothy 2:3–4

Death is one of those huge elephants, lurking in every room, which people simply do not want to think about. Even Christians tend to adopt this attitude, and yet we alone have hope, amid a sea of people who live every moment in genuine danger of everlasting separation from God. We alone hold the secret of salvation and it is our choice whether we keep it concealed from people, or reveal it to as many as we can.

Consider these illustrations: 'If you had the cure for cancer, would you choose to use it?' or 'If you knew how to get out of a burning building, would you choose to share it with others who were trapped with you?' Such scenarios present us with choices which we would consider 'no-brainers', and yet, while none of them comes close to the eternal danger people are in, the choice to share the gospel is not always so obvious.

Of course, this is to be expected. After all, witnessing is really about spiritual warfare - our goal is to seek out those who are enslaved in the kingdom of darkness and show them the way to the kingdom of God. The call to 'Go and make disciples of all nations,' (Matt. 28:19) is a call to go on a rescue mission deep in enemy territory, and as a result we should expect to come under attack from our spiritual enemy. We should expect to be tempted away from sharing the Gospel with people. This is part of the battle we are in, and we need to recognise it as such.

The problem is that, despite the fact that thousands of people who do not know God die every day, and that Jesus gave up His life in the most horrific way imaginable so that we could have the hope of salvation, the enemy's attack is so effective that most of us shy away from sharing this truth.

Even as I am writing this, I am convicted of my own shortcomings as a witness for Christ. I am reminded of the many times I have not passed on the message of salvation and have failed to live in a way that is glorifying to God and demonstrates the truth of the gospel. But my aim here is not to make anyone feel bad about themselves, only to consider how desperate a situation this is, and why this area of spiritual discipline is so vital not only for us, but for those who live around us who do not know God. It's a battle, but it's worth the fight!

We do not have a cure for cancer or the means of escape from a burning building. We have something far, far greater – we have the gospel. 'We are therefore Christ's ambassadors, as though God were making his appeal through us' (2 Cor. 5:20).

> < Reflection

In some countries it is still dangerous to be a Christian, especially if you talk about your faith. People are imprisoned, assaulted and even put to death for such behaviour. It is amazing to think that they are prepared to risk their freedom and wellbeing in such ways.

If you were to let people know you follow Christ and make use of opportunities to tell them the good news, what is the worst that could really happen?

Seen AND Heard

'How, then, can they call on the one they have not believed in? And how can they believe in the one of whom they have not heard? And how can they hear without someone preaching to them?'
Romans 10:14

witnessing

The way we live as followers of Christ is crucial when it comes to being a witness, and no matter how clear and convincing our gospel message might be, if we fail to live in a way that demonstrates the truth of that message it will be emptied of all its power. That said, what we have to say is very important. No matter how holy we are or how much people see that we trust God in all areas of our lives, we must eventually communicate the gospel in words – people do not simply guess the good news!

Our words and our lives work together in declaring our message to the world around us, and there is no limit to our mission field. Our homes, our schools and colleges, our places of work and leisure, and our neighbourhoods all provide us with opportunities to witness. When it comes to getting involved in this mission, here are a few tools I have found helpful:

+ Spend time praying for the people you interact with as you go about your daily life – ask God to help you as you aim to be a good witness to them.

+ Ask God for clear opportunities to be seen and even to be heard as a herald of the gospel, and seize those opportunities when they come.

+ Walk around your own neighbourhood, taking the time to talk to people and getting to know those who live around you.

+ Join a nearby club or society, or 'adopt' a local pub. The aim here is to put yourself in a place where you can be a 'light', so the emphasis is on how you speak, act and generally prove yourself to be someone whose life is shaped by a genuine relationship with God.

+ Be generous with people, especially in your own neighbourhood – offer to lend them your possessions if they are needed, or even give them away.

Obviously this is not an exhaustive list – it's more of a starter for devising your own strategies to get involved in the work of witnessing. Above all, remember that we are not alone in this, but work together with God to spread the gospel.

Application »

As you can probably tell from my handful of witnessing ideas, the main way I go about witnessing is by getting to know people – I enjoy making new friends. The problem comes when, eventually, I try to talk to them about the gospel. I always end up getting muddled and tongue-tied if I have not properly thought it through in my head. It pays to be prepared!

Spend some time working out, and maybe even write down, how you would explain the gospel to someone.

'But you will receive power when the Holy Spirit comes on you; and you will be my witnesses in Jerusalem, and in all Judea and Samaria, and to the ends of the earth.'
Acts 1:8

witnessing

With a name like Phinehas it is no wonder I ended up being teased and bullied at school. There was one boy in particular who picked on me at every opportunity, and so I was not delighted when we were paired up to organise the science room for our school open day. However, when the day came and the two of us started working together on the display, planning things out and getting things set up, we actually got on really well – we even went for a wander round the grounds together. I look back on that as one of the highlights from my school days.

Working together with someone – even someone you do not naturally get along with – can have an amazing effect on your relationship. The same is true when it comes to witnessing. We are not called to the mammoth task of being Christ's witnesses to the ends of the earth on our own. We engage in this work together with God the Holy Spirit. *Our* role is to demonstrate, through both actions and words, the truth of the good news of salvation in Christ and the wonder of having a relationship with God. The Holy Spirit's role is to open people's eyes to this truth, so they can become followers of Jesus themselves.

If we choose *not* to engage in this work with God, we are missing out on a wonderful opportunity to bond with Him and see Him using us to save people.

And though I am a million miles away from being a gifted evangelist, and have often failed in my role as a witness, some of the highest points in my life have involved sharing the gospel with others – especially when I get to see them come to faith in Jesus.

A final important point to bear in mind is that *no* act of witnessing is a failure. We may be laughed at and rejected, get our words muddled and our facts messed up, our lives criticised and end up seeming to put more people off than we draw to God, but our job is not to change people and make them into Christians. Our role is only to be witnesses for God. The rest is up to Him.

> < Reflection

Consider this mind blowing fact: if you are a follower of Christ, the Holy Spirit – God Himself – lives in your body.

Take some time to think about the wonder of this reality, and as you do, remember it is genuinely the reality – even as you think about this, the Holy Spirit is there with you. What a privilege to have the opportunity, just for the few years of our lives, to work together with Him in bearing witness to all that God has done and has promised to do.

witnessing

'In the same way, after supper he took the cup, saying, "This cup is the new covenant in my blood; do this, whenever you drink it, in remembrance of me."'

1 Corinthians 11:25

Jesus is probably best remembered for His death, resurrection and the miracles He performed during His ministry, yet the vast majority of Jesus' time was actually spent preaching the gospel. Matthew tells us that, 'Jesus went throughout Galilee, teaching in their synagogues, preaching the good news of the kingdom' (Matt. 4:23), Mark says, 'Jesus went into Galilee, proclaiming the good news of God' (Mark 1:14), and Luke wrote, 'Jesus travelled about from one town and village to another, proclaiming the good news of the kingdom of God' (Luke 8:1). Not only did Jesus preach the gospel, but it was backed up by His life – His compassion, His miracles and all that He did.

After three years of proclaiming His message, He finally arrived in Jerusalem to fulfil that good news. Here He gathered with His disciples in the upstairs room to eat the Passover meal together, and as He handed them the bread and the wine He referred to them as His body and His blood, so instituting the ritual of communion that we have performed ever since – all so that His followers would not forget Him.

And yet who could possibly forget Him? After the most amazing three years of their lives, and especially witnessing His resurrection, surely not a single one of His disciples was ever going to need reminding about Jesus! And yet the unfortunate truth is that we forget so easily – even the most important of things fade into the background and end up getting overlooked in the hustle and bustle of everyday life.

Communion is an excellent reminder of all that Jesus has done for us, of the joys of having a relationship with God, and the great hope we have for the future. But it is not the only reminder. As we bear witness to the world around us of all that Jesus has done and promised to do for us, we are again reminded of this truth for ourselves. Witnessing helps to keep the wonder of the good news at the forefront of our minds.

This is the message about Jesus, provided through Jesus, and preached by Jesus – He *is* the good news, and He has passed on to us the baton of sharing this message with those who have not heard.

Application »

As we have seen, Jesus did not leave us the task of spreading the message of salvation on our own. We have the Holy Spirit living in us, guiding us and helping us at all times, even at this very moment.

Why not take a little time right now to ask Him to provide you with an opportunity to work with Him through witnessing to someone today? And having done so, look out for that opportunity when it comes ... and take it!

1. Read 2 Timothy 4:5. Even if you are not an 'evangelist', what work is carried out by those who are, and how might you emulate this and so 'do the work' yourself?

2. What excuses, if any, have kept you from sharing the gospel with others? How would you answer these if they were presented by someone else?

3. Read 2 Corinthians 5:20. What similarities might there be between us as Christ's ambassadors and ambassadors in the normal, political sense?

4. Why do you think the way we live as Christians makes a difference to how effective the gospel message is for those around us?

5. Are there aspects of your life that you feel hinder you in your witness for God? How might you go about overcoming these and so becoming a better witness?

6. Read Acts 1:8. We do not engage in this work alone, but do so together with the Holy Spirit. How might this help both in our witness and in our relationship with God?

7. Many of us find the idea of witnessing unappealing, especially when it comes to telling people about Jesus, and so we tend to avoid getting involved in this area of spiritual discipline. How would you explain to another Christian why being a witness is so important and what witnessing actually involves?

witnessing

WEEK 3: FOCUS ON OURSELVES

fasting

Introduction

'When you fast, do not look sombre as the hypocrites do, for they disfigure their faces to show men they are fasting. I tell you the truth, they have received their reward in full.' **Matthew 6:16**

When you fast'! That's a rather bold assumption – almost as if Jesus is expecting His followers to engage in fasting. But why? Consider John Chrysostom, the fourth century preacher, spent a long period of his life standing in the mouth of a cave in wind, rain and snow, without food, water or even sleep, believing this was good for his soul. Unfortunately it was not good for his health and he suffered for the rest of his short life as a result. This is the sort of extreme asceticism that has been associated with fasting in the past, and quite rightly, we tend to shy away from such severe practices. Unfortunately, fasting often ends up being rejected along with everything else.

Fasting is simply not the done thing these days, and while there are some diets that include 'fast days', for the most part society leans toward eating fast food rather than fasting from eating food. How is this austere, ancient custom in any way relevant to us today? And how could fasting ever be of any benefit either physically or spiritually?

As we turn our focus on ourselves in this week of studies, we will be seeking to answer these questions and get to the heart of what fasting is all about.

fasting

'The Ninevites believed God. They declared a fast ... "By the decree of the king and his nobles: Do not let any man or beast, herd or flock, taste anything: do not let them eat or drink."'
Jonah 3:5,7

The Ninevites were evil. So evil, in fact, that Jonah had no desire whatsoever to deliver God's message of impending judgment to them, fearing God might actually have mercy on them! Eventually Jonah delivered the message to the people of Nineveh and the Bible informs us of their response in a typically matter-of-fact way: 'The Ninevites believed God'. The demonstration that followed, however, showed just how serious this belief was. A fast was decreed for all the people, and not only for them but also for their livestock – every man, woman, child and animal in the kingdom was to abstain from food and drink.

Fasting, then, simply involves not eating food or, at times, not drinking either, and the Bible is full of people who engaged in this practice. Queen Esther, for example, called the Jews to fast for three days, neither eating nor drinking (Esth. 4:16). Paul also fasted from food and drink for three days (Acts 9:9). Jesus went for a full forty-day fast from food during His time in the wilderness, while Elijah and Moses added abstinence from water to their forty-day fasts, with Moses immediately embarking on a second fast following the golden calf incident!

We could define this area of spiritual discipline as: *abstaining from that which is necessary for life, which usually means food and sometimes water as well.*

As such, it is important to make a distinction between fasting and abstaining from non-essential things, such as television, chocolate, alcohol or sport. This is not actually fasting at all, but rather the discipline of simplicity (covered elsewhere in this series).

Fasting and simplicity, while they both include some form of abstinence, have very different purposes and effects. Simplicity involves abstaining from potential idols, while fasting involves abstaining from that which is necessary for life. As such, you might add sleep or even air to a list of things you might fast from, but it is probably best to stick to food and, at times, drink.

> < Reflection

When I turn on the tap in my kitchen water comes out. Not only that, but I have a larder and a fridge in my house, and if ever they do not have something I fancy eating there is always the shop around the corner or the supermarket in town. I am never concerned about going hungry or thirsty. And yet we are told that for one in seven people around the world this is not the case. Instead they are starving or suffering from droughts, and they go to bed every night hungry and thirsty.

If God decided to withhold the rain and the sunshine and no longer cause plants to grow, how quickly would we find ourselves in such a situation, too?

Day 2
The Pride of Life

'Is this the kind of fast I have chosen, only a day for a man to humble himself? Is it only for bowing one's head like a reed and for lying on sackcloth and ashes? Is that what you call a fast, a day acceptable to the LORD?'
Isaiah 58:5

By the time of the prophet Isaiah, God's people were not doing well. Although they still had the temple in Jerusalem where they continued to perform various rituals and sacrifices, and they still had their religious feasts and gatherings as the Law prescribed, these displays of devotion masked the reality that their devotion to God was actually sadly lacking. And though they still observed their fasting days, the reason for doing so had long since been replaced with mere ritual and its purpose was not being fulfilled.

There is still confusion over the purpose of fasting, and while most tend not to bother with this area of spiritual discipline at all, many of those who choose to fast do so for the wrong reasons.

The Pharisees used to fast for two days every week, specifically on market days so they could be seen fasting and they made sure people knew they were fasting by appearing scruffy and sad. Jesus told His followers not to fast like the Pharisees, as it had become a source of pride for them, which is about as far away from the purpose of fasting as you can get. The true purpose for fasting is to humble ourselves:

+ 'Yet when they were ill, I put on sackcloth and humbled myself with fasting' (Psa. 35:13).

fasting

+ 'There, by the Ahava Canal, I proclaimed a fast,
  so that we might humble ourselves before our God'
  (Ezra 8:21).

There can be no doubt that God hates pride – not only
because it's listed first among the 'things the LORD
hates' (Prov. 6:16–19), but because of what pride does
to us. 'In his pride the wicked does not seek him; in
all his thoughts there is no room for God' (Psa. 10:4).
Essentially, pride is about thinking more highly of
ourselves than we should, to the point where we feel
no need for God – essentially a proud person becomes
their own god! Fasting, as we will see, is specifically
designed to help keep us humble and remind us of our
complete reliance on God.

> < Reflection

Of what things are you most proud? Academic
achievements or successes at work? Your children or
some particular skill or ability? There is nothing wrong
with being pleased about such things, but the problem
comes when we allow ourselves to start thinking more
highly of ourselves than we ought – this is where *real*
pride begins, and it can quickly lead to us thinking of
others as being inferior and believing that God is less
important and necessary in our lives.

Think again about the things of which you are proud
and consider whether it is you or God who really
deserves the praise.

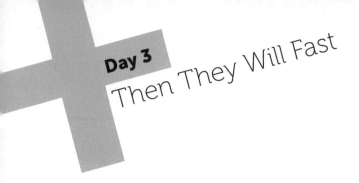

Then They Will Fast

'They said to [Jesus], "John's disciples often fast and pray, and so do the disciples of the Pharisees, but yours go on eating and drinking."'
Luke 5:33

When He was confronted about the lack of fasting among His disciples, Jesus explained that while He was with them there was a temporary hiatus from fasting. However, a day was coming when He would leave this world, and then they would fast. Jesus clearly expected His followers to engage in this area of spiritual discipline. This includes us today.

The practicalities of fasting are fairly straightforward. As we have seen, it involves abstaining from food for a length of time. An 'absolute fast' includes not drinking, which is potentially more physically harmful than only fasting from food – such a fast should never be undertaken for more than three days at a time (as exemplified by Esther and Paul), and then only after seeking God *and* medical advice. For most of us, sticking to a normal fast from food will serve our purpose well.

There are a number of practical considerations that should be taken into account first, though. For example, if you are pregnant, suffer from diabetes or should not abstain from eating for any other reason, fasting from food completely for any length of time is not recommended. This may not necessarily prevent you from engaging in some form of fasting, but you should certainly seek medical advice first.

As for when to fast, this is really between you and God.

fasting

Some people have a couple of days booked in every week, or a few weeks each year, while others are more sporadic, fasting as they feel led to.

A few years ago my wife fasted for ten days, having been prompted by God to do so. I was so amazed she managed it that I immediately, and more in competition than with any sense of God's leading, decided to fast for a full forty days. Why not? I was in some pretty good biblical company! Much to my disappointment I caved in after a mere five days, at which point I stuffed myself so full on burgers that I was quite ill. All I can say is, don't rush into a long period of fasting if you have not fasted for shorter lengths of time first, always end your fast slowly with simple food like fruit and vegetables rather than stuffing yourself on fast food, and don't use fasting as a competition. That said, it wasn't entirely wasted as I was somewhat humbled by the whole experience, which, after all, is its main purpose!

Application ››

Unless there are medical reasons that would prevent you from doing so, try fasting from food for one day this week. Personally I would recommend undertaking the fast from evening to evening (i.e. not eating dinner on the first evening, missing breakfast and lunch, then breaking your fast at dinner on the second evening) but this is entirely up to you.

During your fast, take the time to consider how you feel physically, mentally and spiritually.

By God's Almighty Hand

fasting

'Then I will send rain on your land in its season, both autumn and spring rains, so that you may gather in your grain, new wine and oil. I will provide grass in the fields for your cattle, and you will eat and be satisfied.'
Deuteronomy 11:14–15

As I am writing this, spring is finally kicking in and new life is bursting forth all around. I particularly enjoy watching the crazy antics of lambs in the nearby fields. It is amazing how quickly after being born these gangly, little creatures get up on their feet and start leaping around the place, independent and excitable – so different from human babies. We spend our first months, even years, completely dependent on our parents for everything. And in our relationship with God we are just as, if not more, dependent on Him.

If God did not cause the sun to shine and the rain to fall, if He chose not to let seeds germinate and animals produce offspring, if He caused the rivers and reservoirs to dry up, how long would we survive? When our stomachs are full and satisfied it can be easy to forget that we rely on God for everything. Without His provision we would simply cease to be. In the face of such a reality, can there really be any room for pride? Is there any reason to think that we would be okay without God in our lives?

Fasting provides us with a clear reminder of this fact, and if we allow our hunger to bring us back to the reality of our absolute reliance on God, the goal of fasting will be quickly achieved.

As such, it is important not to get side-tracked into fasting for the wrong reasons. Fasting is not about being prompted to pray, with the hunger pangs acting as a reminder and the lack of meals as extra time for prayer, or about losing weight, at least not when it comes to spiritual discipline, and it is definitely not about twisting God's arm to do our bidding, trying to get Him to eat out of our hands by not eating out of them ourselves.

Fasting is all about humility – reminding ourselves that everything we have comes from God. This helps to keep our relationship well balanced, with us as God's children and Him as our Father, who loves us, cares for us and provides for us.

> < Reflection

In addition to humbling ourselves before God, fasting presents us with a great opportunity to take mastery over our bodies. To deny our bodies something they need in order to survive – and something they will be quick to start demanding – helps us to be disciplined in general.

This is of great importance for us as Christians, just as Paul wrote: '"Everything is permissible for me" – but not everything is beneficial. "Everything is permissible for me" – but I will not be mastered by anything' (1 Cor. 6:12).

A Hunger for God

fasting

> 'For forty days [Jesus] was tempted by the devil. He ate nothing during those days, and at the end of them he was hungry.'
> **Luke 4:2**

As I mentioned previously, I had a stab at a forty day fast, but caved in after a mere five days, by which time I would have eaten my own arms if something more appetising had not presented itself. And yet Jesus went for the full forty days without food while stuck in the fairly hostile environment of the desert. You would think it obvious that after such a mammoth fast Jesus would have been famished, and yet still Luke takes the time to point out that 'He was hungry'! It is a great reminder that Jesus was not simply some sort of superhuman – He had one of these nagging, insistent bodies just like ours, that probably had *Him* considering the gastronomic qualities of His own limbs. And yet He still subjected Himself to over a month without meals, humbling Himself before His Father.

Not long afterwards, when His disciples brought Him food following His conversation with the woman at the well, Jesus told them, 'my food ... is to do the will of him who sent me and to finish his work' (John 4:34), which suggests He often spent time fasting.

If pride is essentially being your own god, Jesus was surely the only person who ever had a right to be proud. And yet, though He is God Himself, He demonstrated ultimate humility. Consider Paul's wonderful description from Philippians 2, where he wrote about Jesus, 'who being in very nature God, did not consider equality with God something to be grasped, but made himself nothing, taking the very nature of a servant, being made in human likeness. And being found in appearance as a man, he humbled himself and became obedient to death – even death on a cross!' (Phil. 2:6–8).

Who could say for certain whether Jesus' fasting had any impact on His humility? But He *did* fast. And He *did* humble Himself before God, relying moment-by-moment on His Father not only for His physical provision, but also for every word He was to say and every action He was to perform.

Application »

'The Didache' is an early Church document detailing how to go about various Christian practices, and it includes the following statement about fasting: 'You should fast on Wednesdays and Fridays.' While this was primarily to avoid fasting on the same days as the Jews, still it prescribed two fast days every week! This direction was not just for priests or monks and the like, but for every member of the church.

Fasting is another of those areas of spiritual discipline that, if it is not planned, simply does not happen. Take the time to consider your weekly schedule and book in regular days of fasting. The frequency is up to you – you do not have to stick with two days a week.

1. How would you explain the difference between fasting and simplicity?

2. Read Hosea 2:5–13. The Israelites believed it was their idols that gave them all they had. It is heart-breaking to read God's words in verse 8: 'she did not know that it was I who gave her the grain, the wine, and the oil' (ESV). Why is it so easy to fall into the trap of thinking what we have comes from sources other than God?

3. If you tried the one day fast (see page 37) what was your experience? If not, why did you choose not to?

4. Have you ever practiced this area of spiritual discipline in the past, and if so, why?

5. What do you believe you would find hardest about fasting, and what steps might you take to help overcome this so you can engage in this area of spiritual discipline?

6. Read Psalm 35:13 and Ezra 8:21. How does fasting help us to humble ourselves before God, and how can we ensure it does not become an opportunity for pride instead?

7. Fasting is considered by many to be an old-fashioned, even barbaric, exercise. How would you explain to either a Christian or a non-Christian the purpose, practice and importance of fasting today?

fasting

WEEK 4: FOCUS ON DAILY LIFE

living for today

Introduction

'Now listen, you who say, "Today or tomorrow we will go to this or that city, spend a year there, carry on business and make money." Why, you do not even know what will happen tomorrow. What is your life? You are a mist that appears for a little while and then vanishes.' **James 4:13–14**

These are typically cheery words from James, reminding us of the brevity and fragility of our lives. Yet despite the slightly melancholic tone, he is making an important point. Planning and even dreaming about the future is very natural for us – not only that but it is often sensible, especially when it comes to our stewardship of the resources God has given us. Can you imagine what a mess you would end up in if you never bothered making any plans or provision for the future?

And yet, at the same time, we are called to focus on one day at a time, leaving the future in God's hands. After all, He might call you home tonight or maybe Jesus will return first, so surely we should live each day as though it could be our last.

As we turn our attention to our daily lives in this final week of studies, we will be looking at the balance between these two attitudes: planning for the future and living for today, together with how and why to engage in this area of spiritual discipline and how it will help to grow our love for God.

The Best Laid Plans …

> 'Therefore do not worry about tomorrow, for tomorrow will worry about itself. Each day has enough trouble of its own.'
> **Matthew 6:34**

living for today

Although I once had a budgie that apparently died of stress, for the most part, birds do not suffer from anxiety or worry – hence the saying, 'free as a bird'. And it was to just such carefree creatures that Jesus pointed when trying to communicate the need for His followers to live for today. Birds do not rush around planting seeds and tending their growth. In the same way, a flower's beauty is not achieved through any work of its own. Instead, God provides for both of them, feeding the birds and adorning the flowers. Though we find this easy enough to accept, and though we are far more important to God than a bird or flower, still we tend to find it hard to trust Him for our own provision.

For non-believers, rushing around worrying and desperately trying to grasp the necessities of life are perfectly natural. Whom else do they have to rely on? But Jesus makes it very clear that we should not be like them: 'do not worry, saying, "What shall we eat?" or "What shall we drink?" or "What shall we wear?" For the pagans run after all these things, and your heavenly Father knows that you need them' (Matt. 6:31–32). We should be different from everyone else because we know God has promised to provide for us. We should live for today, taking one day at a time.

This does not mean, however, that we should not

plan for the future and the Bible is full of people who made good, godly plans – Noah planned the building of his ark, which ensured that life on earth was not entirely extinguished in the flood, Solomon planned the building of God's temple in Jerusalem and Paul planned his missionary journeys around the eastern Mediterranean. We are told that 'a good man leaves an inheritance for his children's children' (Prov. 13:22), which has surely got to take a fair bit of planning! Plans are important. The problem comes when we get so caught up with trying to ensure they come to fruition that we become anxious, and the more powerless we find ourselves to bring them about the more worried we become. In the end, we can spend so much time getting caught up with the future that we fail to enjoy the present.

Living for today, then, does not mean we should ignore the future. Rather it means we should leave the future in God's hands, together with all our hopes, plans and dreams, trusting Him to bring about everything as He desires.

> < Reflection

What plans are most important to you at the moment? What dreams about the future are most insistent in your mind? Imagine if none of those plans ever came to fruition and all your dreams failed to come true. Imagine if all your fears and concerns for the future came to pass instead. How much difference could you really make to such a future by worrying today?

Day 2

Promises! Promises!

living for today

'The one who received the seed that fell among the thorns is the man who hears the word, but the worries of this life and the deceitfulness of wealth choke it, making it unfruitful.'
Matthew 13:22

The Parable of the Sower is well-known in Christian circles, and it is certainly one that I heard preached on many times in my youth and early adulthood. Like many others, I always assumed that the 'seed that fell on good soil' was the one that referred to me – after all, I was a Christian. I had heard and received the message of the kingdom. All I needed to do was sit back and wait for the harvest! It was not until I was reading this passage in my early thirties that I suddenly realised my 'soil' was full of thorns.

This whole parable is about Christian maturity, growing to become more like Christ and deepening in our relationship with God – this is the 'harvest' that we can produce. But our fruitfulness is greatly hindered, and may even be arrested entirely, through worrying and looking for security in worldly things instead of in God.

When calling on His followers to focus on living one day at a time, Jesus gave them a clear promise of provision: 'seek first [God's] kingdom and his righteousness, and all these things will be given to you as well' (Matt. 6:33). 'These things' here refers to everything we need in order to live, exemplified in this passage by food, drink and clothing – God has promised to provide such things for us. Our role, then, is not to go chasing after them, but to seek God's kingdom and righteousness, and His rule and reign in our lives. In short, we are not to pursue the provision, but the person, God Himself.

And God's provision does not stop at only those things we need in order to survive, but He provides us with everything we need in order to serve Him and to live as His people – giving us skills and abilities so we can make a living, providing us with homes and transport, with healthcare and safety. After all, God is not restricted in what He can offer, and Paul promises us that 'my God will meet all your needs according to his glorious riches in Christ Jesus' (Phil. 4:19).

> < Reflection

A few years ago a close friend of mine decided to emigrate to Indonesia, and since he did not want to take all his possessions out there with him, he arranged to store a number of his 'things' in boxes in my loft. When the boxes actually arrived, they ended up taking over a huge amount of space, and apparently this was *after* he had had a good sort out and thrown away most of his stuff!

Have a look around your own home and consider your possessions and provisions. Where did they come from? And, ultimately, who really provided you with all these things?

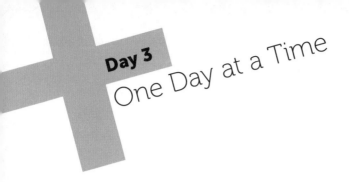

'But if serving the LORD seems undesirable to you, then choose for yourselves this day whom you will serve, whether the gods your forefathers served beyond the River, or the gods of the Amorites, in whose land you are living. But as for me and my household, we will serve the LORD.'
Joshua 24:15

living for today

Living for today does not mean we should abdicate responsibility for making decisions for the future. As we have seen, making plans is not only natural, but important – it only becomes a problem when we start being anxious about whether our plans will come to fruition. Living for today involves making an active, conscious decision to trust God.

In the introduction to this book we saw that spiritual discipline takes lifelong dedication and perseverance. Personally, I find this far too big a challenge to get my head around – even the thought of just one year devoted to spiritual discipline is overwhelming!

The good news is that we do not need to worry about that. Rather, we are called to make the choice *today* to connect with God. Today I will choose to pray. Today I will choose to study the Bible and meditate on what it says. Today I will choose to serve others. Today I will choose to battle temptation. Today I will choose to be disciplined in my life as a follower of Christ. Tomorrow? Who knows what I will choose? But that is not a concern for today.

The need to undertake our lifelong walk with God one day (or even one step) at a time is vital – trying to tackle it as a whole will only result in failure, disappointment and guilt.

Each year, as part of practising simplicity, I try to avoid drinking alcohol in November – somewhat unimaginatively, I call it 'No-alcohol-vember'. I have found that in those years when I allow myself to get overwhelmed by the idea of a whole thirty days' abstinence, I tend to fail within the first week. Yet when I take each of those days one at a time, the task is much easier – or at least that much more achievable. All that my worrying really achieves is failure, because it causes me to lose confidence and give in. This is no less true in my walk with God – even if we live for a hundred years or more, it is still best undertaken one day at a time.

Application »

What things are worrying you at the moment? What cares and concerns are at the forefront of your mind and tend to creep into your thinking without you noticing? Write a list of these things and the reasons they trouble you, and take the time to pray and ask God to take care of them.

Do this every time you think about your concerns today and try to allow yourself to leave them in God's hands – after all, He is the one 'who works out everything in conformity with the purpose of his will' (Eph. 1:11).

'Then the LORD said to Moses, "I will rain down bread from heaven for you. The people are to go out each day and gather enough for that day. In this way I will test them and see whether they will follow my instructions.'
Exodus 16:4

living for today

The area that lies between Egypt and Israel is a hard, barren place, a hostile mixture of desert and mountains, and it was here that the Israelites were forced to wander for forty long years. Bear in mind there would have been hundreds of thousands of them and somehow, in that wilderness, they all needed to eat. In response to their voiced concerns on this subject, God promised to provide them with 'bread from heaven' (aka 'manna'). In His instructions to Moses, God prohibited the people from gathering more than they needed each day – it would not keep but would rot and become maggot-ridden overnight. The Israelites had to trust that God would provide fresh manna each morning, enough for that day.

This daily bread lasted from shortly after leaving Egypt right through to the day Joshua and the people celebrated the Passover in the promised land. Just imagine how this would have shaped the faith of those who experienced this provision, after all, there was now a whole generation who had been raised entirely on this God-given manna.

Although we are not in quite the same situation today, we are still instructed to ask God to 'give us each day our daily bread' (Luke 11:3). Note the emphasis here on today – this is *daily* bread requested *each day,* and this request applies to all we need to get through the day. As Jesus said, 'each day has enough trouble of its own' (Matt. 6:34), and while that sounds like a fairly negative statement, it is delivered with the promise of God's provision. What God is essentially offering us is freedom – freedom from the worries of having to trust worldly things and from the concerns of trying to provide for our future.

Just as communication is vital for building a relationship, if it is really to thrive a relationship has to be built on a solid foundation of trust. Living for today, taking one day at a time in our walk with God, is not easy, but as we take our first, faltering steps of faith and find our Father has not failed us, so we will trust Him more.

> < **Reflection**

The inclination to trust worldly things is very natural. We like to put our faith in things we can see and touch or at least whose track record can be carefully researched and empirically proven. And it is a big emphasis in society – we are called on to trust the government to make good decisions, to trust banks to look after our money, to trust the law to keep us safe, to trust in a healthy lifestyle to ensure long life – and even though their track records are not entirely without blemish, it is all too easy to put our faith in things such as these rather than in God.

Are there things in your own life that you are putting your trust in rather than having faith in God?

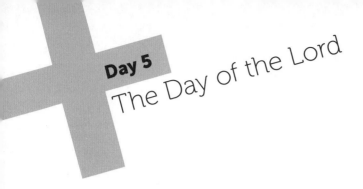

'Jesus replied, "Foxes have holes and birds of the air have nests, but the Son of Man has nowhere to lay his head."'
Matthew 8:20

living for today

As a child, I can remember feeling really sorry for Jesus. It was bad enough that He suffered such a terrible death, but imagine not having a nice, comfy bed to sleep in at night! Throughout His ministry, Jesus spent much of His time travelling up and down the country – He had no wardrobe full of clothes, no handy larder stocked with food, no taps waiting to deliver water at a touch. No home, no income, no obvious possessions. Instead He was reliant on God to provide for Him at all times.

Can you imagine having to live in such a way?

At the same time, Jesus was not haphazard in how He lived and the things He did. Rather, every aspect of His life was meticulously planned (often many hundreds of years in advance!), and He maintained the balance between living for today and planning for the future by looking to God not only for physical provision, but for constant, personal guidance.

In one of His many disputes with the Jews, Jesus told them, 'the Son can do nothing by himself; he can do only what he sees his Father doing, because whatever the Father does the Son also does' (John 5:19). This is taking living for today as far as it can go – living moment-by-moment, looking to God for everything! This is the verse I turn to when people say we should only ask God about the big things, such as looking for a new house, applying to universities, changing career or getting married. Jesus sought God about *everything* – He did nothing without looking to God first. But what about us? How far do we go? Should we ask God what cereal we should have for breakfast, or what shampoo to use? Could such little things really make any difference?

I tested this idea recently when visiting my old hometown. While my wife and children were playing in the park, I went to find a coffee, and as I left the park I had a choice of turning left or right. It seemed a fairly trivial choice, but I asked God which way to go and settled on going left. On my way I bumped into an old school friend who was struggling with having just heard that his father was dying. We spent a good while chatting together and I even took the opportunity to pray for him – an opportunity I would have missed had I turned right!

Far from being a waste of our's or God's time, surely looking to Him for constant guidance and provision can only be of *benefit* both in our relationship with Him and for the kingdom.

Application »

No matter how impractical it might appear, try today, as often as you can remember, to run every decision past God, no matter how small.

1. Read Proverbs 13:22, Matthew 6:34 and Ephesians 1:11. How do you reconcile the need to plan for the future with the call to live for today?

2. There is a natural tendency to want to rely on worldly things and find security in them rather than in God. Why do you think this is the case?

3. Read Matthew 6:25–34. Why is worrying and 'running after all these things' such a natural reaction, and how can this be countered by faith in a practical way?

4. Corrie Ten Boom said, 'Worry does not empty tomorrow of its sorrow. It empties today of its strength'. Why is worrying so discouraged for Christians and how does it relate to trusting in God?

5. How can we balance the call to keep ourselves from worrying about the necessities of life while also providing for ourselves and those in our care?

6. In John 5:19, Jesus said He could do nothing unless He had sought God's guidance first. How might we apply this same principle to our lives and what might be the benefits or difficulties of such a lifestyle?

7. Jesus told us not to worry about life's necessities, because that is how people behave who do not know God. If you came across a believer who worried about such things, how would you explain to them why living for today is important for Christians? How might we put it into practise?

living for
today

Leader's notes:

These notes are designed to help with the 'Questions for Consideration or Discussion' and may be used for individual study or for leading these sessions in a group.

Introductory Questions – page 6

1. While these verses may appear to suggest that our salvation (i.e. 'what God has promised' and 'the crown of life') depends on our perseverance, this does not mean that we can lose our salvation. It is important to bear in mind that salvation is more than getting to go to heaven, but also includes everything that comes with salvation – our relationship with God, our transformation to becoming more like Christ, our witness to the world around us and so on, all of which require perseverance.

2. to 5. It may be worth writing down what you understand to be the purpose and practice of these four areas of discipline. It does not need to be an exhaustive description, maybe just a list of bullet points or a couple of sentences. You can then refer back to these in the next few weeks to see if your understanding of these has changed.

6. The focus here is specifically on your experience of these four areas of spiritual discipline. If you are leading a small group, sharing personal examples may encourage others to share as well.

7. The aim here is to demonstrate that all relationships need to be worked at, not just marriage or our relationship with God. And if it is true of *all* relationships, no matter how great a role they play in our lives, then it must also be true of the greatest one of all – our relationship with God.

Week 1: Prayer – page 18

1. Despite being simple in theory, prayer is hard in practice. Try to go through the whole process, including preparation, location, speaking and listening, as you consider your own experiences of prayer.

If you are leading a small group, it is worth being ready to share first to encourage others to participate.

2. This builds on the previous question and should be tackled subjectively as well as objectively.

3. The terms Jesus uses to describe the Holy Spirit's work are: teach, remind, guide, speak and tell. This question is really about your own experience of the Holy Spirit's communication with you – in question 5 you will consider how to recognise His voice.

4. Some conditions to God granting prayer can be found in the following verses: Matthew 18:19, Mark 11:24, John 14:14 & 15:7, James 4:3 and 1 John 5:14.

When it comes to our relationship with God, consider the requests children make to their parents. Whether these are granted depends on the will of the parents, but this does not mean the requests are not worthwhile. The alternative is for children to *only* ask for things against their parents' will, or to make no requests at all – both of which would be detrimental to their relationship.

5. It is important to bear in mind that this verse is not saying that if you find it hard to recognise God's voice then you do not belong to Him. Rather it is making the point that we can trust God to guide us. There were a few suggestions about learning to recognise His voice on pages 12 and 13.

prayer

If you are leading a small group it may be worth writing down ideas that are shared so a copy can be given to everyone.

6. We spend a huge amount of our lives in thought – conducting an internal monologue in our heads. Christian meditation includes involving God in our general thinking, which could well include talking to and listening to Him.

7. There is a saying, 'you don't really know something unless you can explain it', and each set of questions ends with a similar challenge to explain the practice and purpose of the discipline being considered.

The aim of this question is to ensure you have a proper understanding of prayer; thinking how you would explain this to a non-Christian means assuming a general lack of biblical knowledge and understanding of Christian jargon.

If you are part of a small group, it may be worth turning this into a role-playing exercise so each person gets to explain the purpose of prayer to another.

Week 2: Witnessing – page 30

1. Most local churches have at least one person who is known as an 'evangelist'. Even if you do not know such a person, try to come up with a list of the things people might do as they carry out their evangelistic work. These could include starting conversations with people they don't know, working comments and questions about Christianity into the conversation, and carrying evangelistic tracts with them.

2. Here are a number of classic excuses:

+ 'I have no non-Christian friends.'

+ 'I do not have the gift of evangelism.'

+ 'I do not have enough time.'

+ 'I am afraid of what people will think of me.'

+ 'People can figure it out themselves as long as I live out my faith in front of them.'

+ 'I never know how to bring up the topic.'

+ 'I am worried I might be asked a question to which I do not know the answer.'

+ 'My local church is not really into evangelism.'

Considering your own excuses from someone else's point of view may help to work through how to tackle them.

3. In general, ambassadors represent their own country while living as a foreigner elsewhere. As such, everything they do reflects on their home country and

witnessing

so they tend to live in a way that is not only as upright as possible, but exemplifies their country's typical way of life. This is not a million miles away from how we have been called to live as citizens of heaven!

4. The answer to this may seem obvious, but it is worth taking some time over this discussion starter as this is a really important issue.

5. This builds on the previous question, taking the opportunity to consider our own lives as Christ's ambassadors. The aim is not to beat ourselves up, but to make an honest assessment of how we live then to focus on the 'overcoming' aspect of this discussion starter.

If you are leading a small group discussion, it is worth being prepared to share examples from your own life, as some people may feel uncomfortable about discussing things they feel hinder their witness for God.

6. On pages 26 and 27 we looked at the division of labour, with our role being to bear witness to the gospel and the Holy Spirit's being to open people's eyes to the truth. First consider how understanding our role can help us to witness, then how working together with God will help to develop our relationship with Him.

7. By trying to convince a fellow Christian, you can assume they have at least some sense of the importance of witnessing.

If you are part of a small group (or partnership) try role playing this situation – trying to answer some of the excuses raised in question 2 may help.

Week 3: Fasting – page 42

1. On page 33 we saw that, although both involve some form of abstinence, in fasting we abstain from food and drink – those things which are essential for life – while in simplicity it is from those things that may be, or become, idols in our lives.

2. It is worth taking the time to look at your own possessions and provisions, and consider what or who you tend to think of as being the source of these things. Even something as simple as a loaf of bread has a number of possible choices – including the person who paid for it, or the shop where it was bought, the bakery who produced it or the farmer who grew the wheat.

I tend to get easily tricked into thinking that I provide for my family through earning money, but ultimately even my ability to work is a gift from God!

3. If you did the fast day, try to think about as many aspects of the experience as possible, from the feelings of hunger to any sense of being reminded that God is the ultimate provider of all things. If you did not do the fast, consider seriously your reasons for not doing so, listing all that come to mind as this may help you to engage in this area of spiritual discipline.

4. The aim here is to analyse the motivation behind any previous fasts (especially if undertaken for periods longer than a single day).

If you are leading a small group, take the time to consider your own experiences and be prepared to share these to encourage others.

fasting

5. The obvious answer to this question is that being hungry or thirsty, or even the idea of it, can put us off fasting. However, it is worth considering this in greater depth to see if there is more to fasting that you would find difficult.

If you did not do the fast day, your reasons from question 3 may help.

6. Try first to come up with clear definitions for 'humility' and 'pride' (not necessarily the dictionary definitions).

Consider Jesus' warnings about fasting like the 'hypocrites' in Matthew 6:16–18. While not telling others when we are fasting can help keep this practice from making us feel proud, the fact that we so quickly become hungry (and grouchy, if you are anything like me!) should remind us of our complete reliance on God for everything.

7. When considering how you would explain fasting to a Christian, imagine they do not understand the purpose of this practice for God's people today. If you were explaining to a non-Christian, on the other hand, imagine they associate fasting with an ancient and unknown form of religion.

Again, if you are leading a small group, get people to role-play this exercise.

Week 4: Living for Today –

page 54

1. These three verses talk about the need to plan for the future, the call to focus on today and the fact that God is sovereign in all things. The aim of this discussion starter is to work out if it is really possible to maintain a balance between planning for tomorrow and living for today.

2. Spend some time thinking about any worldly things you rely on or find security in, such as banks and businesses, friends and family members, or physical health and exercise. Then consider whether, in certain areas, you tend to trust these things *more* than you trust God.

3. Building on the previous question, the aim is to work out why we seek to be independent from God (not as a conscious decision, of course), and how we can ensure we remain dependent on Him. Bear in mind what we saw in the previous week of studies about pride and becoming our own gods – humility and reminding ourselves of the reality of our complete dependence on God play a vital role in living for today.

4. It is worth reading the Parable of Sower and Jesus' explanation in Luke 8:5–8 and 11–15. Bear in mind that the fruitfulness here is primarily referring to our Christian maturity, which is undermined as a result of worrying.

5. The Bible is clear that we should take responsibility for providing for ourselves and those in our care – we cannot expect to sit back and wait for food and other necessities to simply appear. The problem arises

living for today

when, as we spend our time and energy providing for ourselves and others, our trust in God's provision is undermined. The aim of this discussions starter is to consider how we work to provide for ourselves and others, while also remaining dependent on God.

6. If you tried the application on page 33, the experience may help as you consider this question. It can be very easy to focus on the perceived difficulties of seeking God's guidance in every decision, so make sure you give at least as much time to thinking about the possible benefits, both for your relationship with God and your decision-making process in general.

7. As with the final questions in the previous weeks, the aim here is to make sure you can communicate clearly and consistently the importance of living for today and how it is possible to do so.
Again, if you are leading a small group it may be worth turning this into a role-playing exercise.

Courses and seminars

Publishing and new media

Conference facilities

Transforming lives

CWR's vision is to enable people to experience personal transformation through applying God's Word to their lives and relationships.

Our Bible-based training and resources help people around the world to:

- Grow in their walk with God
- Understand and apply Scripture to their lives
- Resource themselves and their church
- Develop pastoral care and counselling skills
- Train for leadership
- Strengthen relationships, marriage and family life and much more.

Our insightful writers provide daily Bible-reading notes and other resources for all ages, and our experienced course designers and presenters have gained an international reputation for excellence and effectiveness.

CWR's Training and Conference Centres in Surrey and East Sussex, England, provide excellent facilities in idyllic settings – ideal for both learning and spiritual refreshment.

CWR, Waverley Abbey House,
Waverley Lane, Farnham,
Surrey GU9 8EP, UK

Telephone: **+44 (0)1252 784700**
Email: info@cwr.org.uk
Website: www.cwr.org.uk

Registered Charity No 294387
Company Registration No 1990308